John

The Life and Times
of the Curé d'Ars

by
J. B. Midgley

*All booklets are published thanks to the
generous support of the members of the
Catholic Truth Society*

CATHOLIC TRUTH SOCIETY
PUBLISHERS TO THE HOLY SEE

Contents

Patron of parish priests

Pope John Paul II reminded the Church that the Mass is central to Catholic life and that participation in the Sacrifice demonstrates Catholic identity. The ministerial and hierarchical priesthood is therefore in the closest relationship with the Eucharist, and this is the reason for the Sacrament of Priesthood that protects the mystery of Faith. He also identified the re-evangelisation of Europe as the major challenge of the twenty-first century, and urged a rediscovery of common spiritual roots, Christianity's indisputable and unequalled contribution to European culture and civilisation, and the enduring wisdom of Christian heritage. (cf. *The Holy Eucharist*, 1980 and *The Church in Europe*, 2003)

In his very first encyclical, Pope Benedict XVI observes that "the lives of the saints are not limited to their earthly biographies, but continue being and working in God after death. They do not withdraw from men, but rather become truly close to them. Like the Blessed Virgin Mary, they love every generation with a benevolence that results from intimate union with God, through which the soul is totally pervaded by Him, a condition which enables those who have drunk from the fountains of God's love to become, in their turn, a fountain from which 'flow rivers of living water'" (Encyclical, *God is Love*, 2005).

John Vianney is the patron saint of Parish Priests and the only one to be canonised. In her human manifestation, the Church is passing through an era when, again priests undertake their parish mission single-handed, and when reduced attendance and shortage of vocations threaten parishes with closure or amalgamation. John Vianney's story illustrates the essential excellence of the priesthood upon which Christians depend, and it seems an appropriate time to avail ourselves of his eager intercession with confidence.

Downham Market, Advent 2007

Formative Years

The Vianney family

The first half of the eighteenth century was not a happy time for France. The reigns of Louis XIV and Louis XV saw both secular and clerical efforts to release the Church from Roman control with unprofitable results. Lavish expenditure in high places and unlimited privileges for the affluent, drove the working and rural classes into increased taxation, and desperation. Compared to the growing prosperity of England, Holland, and other European countries, France's stature in the world was diminishing as she relinquished her hold on India, surrendered Canada, and struggled to sustain a share in maritime trade. Her kings and aristocracy may have been complaisant, but her people were miserable, felt excluded from any say in government, resentful of inequality, and increasingly rebellious.

The Vianney family was a splendid example of the farming stock that had provided the backbone of the country. For generations, they had held their farm that lay on either side of the river Rances at Dardilly, a pleasant, well-wooded village in the Rhone province about eight miles from Lyons, a major city of central France. In 1770 the head of the family was Pierre Vianney who was not wealthy, but was able to give them security, shelter, warmth, plenty of food, and a healthy if hardworking life style. He had not yet felt the impact of circumstances that would bring revolution, but was well aware of the increasing number of the poor and socially neglected who wandered from village to village in search of work or alms. He did everything he could to reduce their suffering with his hospitality, and among their guests was the ascetic and ubiquitous pilgrim to the sacred shrines of Europe, Saint Benedict Joseph Labre, 1748-1783. Like the others, he was given a bowl of soup and a night's shelter in the barn for which he wrote a letter of thanks that was treasured by the family. On 11th February, 1778, Pierre's son Matthieu Vianney married Marie Beluse of nearby Ecully. The third of their six children was born at midnight on May 8th 1786, and in the morning was baptised Jean-Baptiste-Marie, but let us hereafter call him John.

Revolution, terror and persecution

Pierre was an exemplary Catholic and his wife Marie a model of religious conviction and piety, with a love of prayer that she transmitted to her children. Even as an infant, John reached firm conclusions about right and wrong, did not hesitate to give others the benefit of his observations, and remained forever grateful for his mother's teaching and influence. Pius VI, who had been elected Pope in 1775, was confronted by growing nationalism, secularism, and atheism that caused more tension between Church and State. Louis XVI was kindly disposed and wanted to do what was right, but he had little understanding of his people's problems and was not well served by his advisers. It was inevitable that as the situation deteriorated, the beleaguered populace should rise in revolt. John was only three when the French Revolution erupted and introduced a Reign of Terror that did not end until 1791 when Robespierre was executed, and the rule of the French Republic passed to the group called the Directory that held sway until the arrival of Napoleon.

The Revolutionaries had adopted an anticlerical programme that led to the closure of churches unless they were served by priests who swore allegiance to a State Church. Those who refused to accept the Civil Constitution of the Clergy went into hiding, were deported, or executed, and members of religious orders were persecuted to the extent that many disguised themselves or escaped to elsewhere in Europe. The Reign of Terror in Paris touched even Dardilly where intrepid Catholics like the Vianneys went to remote farms visited by loyal priests who risked their lives to celebrate Mass for the faithful and administer the Sacraments. It is not surprising that in John's mind the practice of the Faith and fidelity to the Church became associated with the persevering heroism he witnessed and was to emulate so nobly.

John's formative years

As soon as he was about six years of age, John was considered old enough to help his father on the farm, herding the sheep and cattle and tilling the soil. He was a model of obedience, and worked hard in a demanding routine that was nurturing a remarkable capacity for physical endurance that would stand him in good stead. He seemed to have little interest in the games and make-believe pursuits of the young, and preferred involvement in matters relating to the Church. He was always conscious of the presence of God and years later recalled, "When I was alone working in the fields, I would pray aloud, but in my heart if others were there. Happy days! If I hit my hoe or spade in the ground I would say, 'In this way I must cultivate my soul, plucking out evil weeds, and preparing it for the good seed of the good God.'" He was delighted to be involved in his parents' continuing hospitality to the poor, denied himself so as to make his own contribution, and if any children were there he would encourage them to pray, but always so charmingly that none ever took offence. When he was nine, he had the chance to spend a brief period in the little school that had opened in the village. He did not hesitate to share what he learned with others, give them his positive views on responsibility to the Church, and share his own pious inclination to prayer. A year later Napoleon invaded the Papal States, forced the Pope to surrender a substantial section of territory, along with precious works of art and manuscripts, and exacted his formal recognition to the new French Republic.

In 1799, Pius VI was driven from Rome by Napoleonic forces, died in exile, and was succeeded by the Benedictine Pope Pius VII, 1800-1823. He had to lead the Church in coming to terms with a new philosophical, political, and scientific movement, now remembered as the 'Enlightenment', brought into being by European philosophers like Diderot, Rousseau and Kant who developed and popularised the earlier thinking of Newton, Hobbs, Locke, Descartes, and Spinoza with the intention of reforming society. It was characterised by an overconfident assessment of human reason, an optimistic view of human nature, passionate advocacy of its freedom, and an antipathy for tradition, religion, the supernatural, and all authority other then that which was based on reason. Although it had more influence on Protestantism, 'Enlightenment' focused the minds of Catholic Church leaders on the humanitarian ideals of tolerance, equality and freedom in social reform, and the influence of developments in science and technology.

Renewed attention was given to the Biblical and theological scholarship that was to accommodate scientific progress, humanitarian ideals influencing social reform, the quality of education, including that of the clergy, and the eradication of superstition that masqueraded as religion.

First holy communion

The thirteen year old John was now prepared for his First Holy Communion in Ecully, where his maternal grandfather still lived, by two Sisters of the Order of Saint Charles who, like so many other brave religious, had hidden themselves in secular dress to preserve their vocation and its purposes. He first received the Blessed Sacrament at a secret Mass celebrated in a house in Ecully behind windows that were shuttered so that no candlelight could be detected from out side. Some relief came with the Concordat of 1802 when Napoleon allowed Pius VII to re-establish the Catholic Church in France on condition that he replaced the existing hierarchy with new appointments, and provided he accepted that the Church's importance was secondary to that of the State. The relationship remained problematic but Napoleon found it politically expedient to acknowledge Papal authority, an admission that proved helpful to its exercise. Pius was able to oppose secularising, 'enlightened' modernity with vigour, encourage the education of the clergy, and make Rome a centre of culture by restoring and opening new museums, and building schools to expand the education system.

New purpose for Church

Despite persecution, bloodshed and terror, the Revolution had brought one benefit to the Church in France. Her feudal, hierarchical, and mediaeval characteristics had so diminished that clergy and faithful now looked to Rome and the Pope for protection, a change of heart history describes as 'Ultramontinism', 'beyond the mountains'. Stripped of wealth and power, the Church in France now concentrated on her fundamental mission to preach the Gospel and serve the people in fidelity to Apostolic teaching. There was a return to the traditional Catholic values, and an intellectual appreciation of the Church as the Mother of art and Guardian of patriotism. The Romanticism in literature and art that added an appreciation of emotion, intuition, individualism, and history to the Enlightenment's emphasis on classicism and reason, generated a fresh evaluation of the attitudes and values of previous eras, a cautious attitude towards speculative theology, and a reliance on Rome for authoritative answers to all questions.

Vocation

1804 was memorable for two events. In Paris, Napoleon crowned himself Emperor in the Pope's presence, and John Vianney first told his father that he felt called to the priesthood. It seems that at the time Mathieu could not manage without his son's help, and another two years passed before John could enter the "presbytery school" that had been founded at Ecully by Father Bellay who was the parish priest there. This saintly and learned man, who had bravely ministered to his flock despite the Reign of Terror, was so committed to the pastoral ministry that he had declined the offer of a professorship at the Seminary of Saint Irenaeus in Lyons. He was the first to whom John confided his longing to devote himself entirely to the glory of God and the salvation of souls.

Priesthood

Preparation at Saint Sulpice

The Seminary of Saint Irenaeus in John's diocese came under the administrative and philosophical aegis of the mother-house of Saint Sulpice that has served the Church with a benign purpose that is still relevant. In 1641, Father Jean Jacques Olier, the parish priest of Saint Sulpice in Paris, assembled a group of like-minded clergy who were eager to dedicate themselves to the religious and intellectual formation of candidates for the priesthood. The community lived in a house attached to the church where they opened the first seminary of the Society of Saint Sulpice. As patron they adopted Sulpicius (d.647), a beloved Bishop of Bourges renowned for protecting his people from tyranny, caring for the afflicted, and whose death brought forth a remarkable outpouring of grief and veneration. The French School of Spirituality was distinguished by devotion to the Blessed Virgin Mary, Mother of God, so it was only natural and appropriate that she should be honoured as the Patroness of the seminary where "a most filial confidence and tender devotion were the characteristic of the house."

The Founder wanted to help aspirants to the priesthood to be holy and cultured men who were expert in the knowledge that their incomparable mission required. "Care must be taken", he wrote, "that there is nothing wanting in the instruction of clerics regarding doctrine and piety. The Society of Saint Sulpice will provide instruction for each one according to his ability in Philosophy, Scholastic and Moral Theology, and Polemics. In the pulpit, the priest must speak for the learned as well as the ignorant, uphold the truths of the Gospel, combat vice, resist the torrent of prevailing opinion, and confound heresy. Unmasking subterfuge and what is false requires a deeper and wider knowledge than that acquired by private study, a knowledge to be tested in the schools and academies." For this reason, his seminarians attended courses at the University of the Sorbonne that was then a stronghold of uncontaminated faith and a bastion against Jansenism.

Cornelius Jansen, 1585-1638, was a Flemish theologian, Bishop of Ypres, and dedicated student of Saint Augustine of Hippo whose treatise *Augustinus* was published in 1640, two years after his death. Unfortunately it carried Augustine's theology too far, by advocating a rigorous spirituality that attempted to stifle human nature that was regarded as essentially corrupt. The ideas offered on grace and free will were more like the Protestant belief in the sufficiency of grace than the Catholic teaching that humans must cooperate with God's grace through good works. The emphasis on the irresistible character of grace undervalued free will, a severe morality was recommended, and the chances of salvation viewed with pessimism. Jansenism attracted a strong following, especially in France, so its condemnation by Pope Innocent X in 1653, was seen by French Catholics as an affront to their independence and integrity. In the ensuing tension, a national movement with theological overtones asserted that papal authority could be exercised only through a General Council to which its decrees must be subject.

Father Olier believed that "God's plan for the reform of the Church was to secure the young by teaching them Christian principles and inculcating the fundamental maxims of salvation." On Sundays and the major Feasts, therefore, the seminarians taught Catechism to the children of the parish and beyond. The Sulpicians regarded themselves as educators as well as guardians of souls, and followed a schedule of prayer, spiritual conferences and study. Their Society became identified with the revival of parish life, the reform of seminary education, the nourishment of the spiritual life of the clergy, and inspired saints like John Eudes and John Baptist de La Salle.

Conscription

John's previous educational opportunities had been so slender that it is not surprising that he encountered difficulty with his studies, particularly Latin. The average age of his fellow pupils at the presbytery school was about twelve, but this embarrassment did not lessen the twenty year old's resolve to answer God's call, and he persevered with the constant support and example of Father Bellay who recognised his extraordinary qualities. As a theology student in the Archdiocese of Lyons he was entitled to exemption from military service but, by some administrative oversight, he was called up in 1809 to join Napoleon's armies in Spain. He was ordered to join his regiment at Bayonne, but on the way he fell ill and had to be taken to hospital in Lyons. He was barely convalescent when he was conscripted again and told to report at Roanne. This time, he failed to join the departing unit because he was deep in prayer at the church. He made a valiant but fruitless effort to catch up with his comrades, was befriended by a sympathetic deserter, and for some months worked on a farm where he also gave some rudimentary lessons to the children who lived there. It was fortunate that a few months later Napoleon, on the occasion of his marriage in 1810 to Archduchess Marie-Louise, declared an amnesty for deserters and defaulters, and John was able to return to Ecully and resume his studies.

A struggling student

In the autumn of 1812, John entered the preparatory seminary of Verrieres near Montbrison and received the tonsure. Continued problems with his studies and poor results in the regular examinations caused some younger fellow students to tease him, but he bore this with good humour, and no one doubted his consistent piety and noble qualities. When things were particularly difficult, he found great comfort in praying to the Jesuit, Saint John Francis Regis, 1597-1640, who had spent his priestly life in ceaseless missionary work in his native France, bringing back many who had abandoned the faith during the Wars of Religion, visiting prisons, assisting the poor and opening homes for the rehabilitation of prostitutes.

Ordination

When John progressed to the major Seminary of Saint Irenaeus, he did so badly in the theology examination that he was asked to leave, and was saved only by the reputation of Father Bellay who stepped in and promised to give him private tuition. John still failed the written examinations in May, but Father Bellay managed to persuade the Rector to test him orally. John did well, and the Vicar General, Monsignor Courbon who was administering the diocese in the absence of Cardinal Feshi, decided that the candidate's shining piety more than compensated for his unfamiliarity with Latin. John was duly ordained sub-deacon on 2nd July, 1814, by Bishop Simon of Grenoble, and went on to complete his final year's study under Father Bellay's supervision. He received the diaconate on 23rd June, 1815, five days after Napoleon's downfall at the battle of Waterloo. The date for his ordination to the priesthood was fixed for August 13th, and this meant he had to walk the eighty miles from Ecully to Grenoble through territory swarming with Austrian troops. When he arrived, some senior clergy were embarrassed that he was the only ordinand that day, but the perceptive Bishop Simon said "It's not any trouble to ordain a good priest."

Curate to Father Bellay

After ordination and the joyful celebration of his first Mass, John was appointed curate to Father Bellay who had helped him so much on his journey to the priesthood. The knowledge that he had absorbed from the lectures delivered in Latin in Saint Irenaeus' Seminary was minimal, and he relied on a handy reference manual called the *Rituel de Toulon* that provided helpful summaries of Dogmatic and Moral Theology. In Father Bellay, he was again blessed with an erudite personal tutor who patiently and so successfully widened his knowledge and comprehension of Moral Theology that his faculties as a confessor were granted within a couple of months. Almost immediately, he demonstrated remarkable qualities in the confessional where he gave earnest and encouraging advice to those who came to the Sacrament of Penance and Reconciliation in increasing numbers. Though he was not very eloquent, the congregation was always appreciative and attentive when he preached.

Growing reputation

Father Bellay wore a hair shirt and ate very little, an example followed by his curate who obtained a similar garment, wore a band with spikes on the inside on his left arm, and copied his diet of a few unsavoury potatoes. It is recorded that, "Out of kind concern, each drew the Vicar General's attention to the other's excessive mortification in their race to holiness"! John was at Ecully for the best part of three years, carrying out the heavier parochial duties and continuing his studies. He was grief-stricken when his beloved Parish Priest died in December 1817. He said of him, "He died like a saint as he was, and his pure soul departed to add new joy to Paradise." It says much about John's growing reputation and popularity that the Ecully parishioners petitioned Monsignor Corbon, for him to succeed as Parish Priest, but the Vicar General had other plans in mind.

Parish Priest of Ars

Early in February 1818, Monsignor Corbon asked John to come and see him. "Thirty miles from here, my dear friend," he told him, "in the district of Trevoux, the village of Ars-en-Dombe is without a Curé. The church there is a chapel of ease serving about two hundred souls. There's not much love of God in this village. Your job will be to instil it." The Vicar General was renowned as a splendid judge of character and, in this case, confidence was again well placed. This unprepossessing place is about twenty miles from Lyons and ten miles east of the main Lyons-Paris road so, in those days and even now, one would need a special reason to make a visit. Although John had few possessions to carry, it was a wearisome walk, and he was glad to talk with a young boy who helped him with directions as he neared his destination. "You have shown me the way to Ars," he said gratefully, "and I will show you the way to heaven." When he caught sight of the village, he fell to his knees, wisely invoked his Guardian Angel, and went straight to the church. First impressions were not encouraging. The building was just a narrow nave with no side chapels, the altar was shabby, the Tabernacle empty, and the sanctuary lamp not lit. The steeple had been vandalised by revolutionaries, and the single bell dangled perilously between two insecure props, but this did not deter him the next morning from ringing it himself for the Angelus before celebrating Mass. Only a few parishioners turned up, and some of these only out of curiosity.

A thoroughly neglected flock

The parish was still recoiling from the effects of the French Revolution that had resulted in a shortage of priests and a dramatic decline in Mass attendance. John's parishioners had not lost their Faith but had become careless in its practice

He identified the problems confronting him as ignorance of the teachings of the Church, disregard of Sunday observance by unnecessary labour, pleasure seeking, excessive drinking, dancing which he regarded as an occasion of sin even for onlookers, immodest dress, blasphemy, profanity and obscenity. He lost no time in denouncing these from the pulpit, and then made a personal visit to every home and family, taking details of all the children and immediately arranging catechism classes for them.

Prayer and self-denial

His unwavering faith in God's providence gave him a certainty that his flock would return to traditional practice of the Faith if he himself did penance on their behalf. With earnest exhortation and the example of his own prayer and self-denial, he was going to inspire a new fervour. He began by giving his mattress to a beggar and took to sleeping either on the floor or on a pallet on the bed with a log for a pillow. He still wore his hair shirt and the spiked band on his arm, scourged himself and, if he bothered to eat at all, it was a few unsavoury potatoes at midday. He slept only a few hours, rose at midnight and went to the church to recite the Divine Office, and remained kneeling there without support until it was time for him to say morning Mass. He gave generously to the poor, not from his surplus but from what he needed, mended his clothes himself and, having been given a present of a new pair of breeches, immediately exchanged them with a beggar's.

He maintained that if suffering were accepted properly and willingly, it would be rewarded even in this life. Years later he said to a colleague who was despondent about the lukewarm attitude of his parishioners, "You've preached, you've prayed, but have you fasted? Have you scourged yourself? Have you slept on bare boards? If not, you have no reason to complain." In addition to his own penitential self-denial and preaching, he gave every attention to the importance and dignity of the Liturgy and appropriate ritual. While his cassocks were always threadbare, he bought the finest vestments he could find in Lyons and purchased a new high altar from his own slender resources.

Straight talking

John preached every morning, longer on Sundays, and the initially small congregation of Sunday worshippers found that his positive style made a gentle nap impossible. They knew that when he took off his chasuble to go into the pulpit they would be in for an hour when they would hear little for their comfort as he fearlessly reproved the drunken behaviour, dancing, immodest dress, and working on Sundays to which the citizens of Ars seemed particularly prone. Personal austerity inclined him to speak about death, judgement and hell, and he was so dedicated to saving souls that details of moral teaching were presented without compromise so that the least learned in his congregation would understand. He believed that, "if a pastor wishes to avoid damnation, he must, if there is a scandal in the parish, overcome motives of human respect and the fear of being hated or despised by the parishioners; and even if he were certain of being killed when he left the pulpit, that must not stop him." He preached what he believed people living in the nineteenth century needed to know for their spiritual development, and soon they realised that if he was uncompromising in the sermon, he was the soul of gentleness in conversation, and that his intention was to lead them to the joys of Heaven.

Some effects of Jansenism had survived in the rigour of tone and detail with which dogma was presented, so it was natural that John spoke to his people in the language they had grown to understand in the context and practices of the time. Habitual and public sin was castigated, and there was a strict approach in matters relating to the Sacraments of the Holy Eucharist and Penance. Emphases and explanations may develop at particular times, and modern attitudes to, for example, fasting, parish dances, lotteries, public houses, and theatres are more flexible than in the nineteenth century. As far as John was concerned, the important thing to remember is that the truth of Catholic theology remains constant.

Demonic visitations

Battles were not won overnight. Some of the disaffected raised a petition to have John moved, saying that he was an awful priest. He agreed with their assessment and signed it himself! Others, angry that their pleasures were interrupted and curtailed, went so far as to try and ruin his good name by false allegations of immorality, or resorted to physical abuse and attempted intimidation. Although the wicked lies were exposed, they caused him great heartache to which was added the disturbance of his brief sleep by fiendish manifestations of the devil himself, appearing under different guises - a phenomenon which was very real, and from which he would emerge bruised and exhausted. Chairs in his room were pushed about, curtains ripped, and his bed dragged across the floor to the accompaniment of the noise of howling dogs. He endured these visitations with a smile, saying that they were invariably the prelude to the conversion of some poor sinner. In time, the dancing and wild drinking stopped, though much to the disgruntlement of the innkeepers! Sunday observance was restored, villagers no longer cursed, swore, or cheated one another by giving false measure in their dealings, and when the Bishop made his visitation he found the children to be the best instructed in the diocese.

Dedicated Preacher

Influences on his thinking and spirituality

The seventeenth century had witnessed a significant Catholic revival thanks in large measure to Cardinal Pierre de Berulle, 1575-1629. He is rightly honoured as the founder of the distinctive French School of Spirituality that further blossomed with contributions of such luminaries as Saint Francis de Sales, d.1622, and Saint Vincent de Paul, d.1660, and was to remain an exemplary influence in the Church until the twentieth century. He was the most eminent theologian, writer and spiritual director of his day, was concerned for the reform and education of the clergy and, following the example of Saint Philip Neri, 1515-1595, founded the French Congregation of the Oratory for that purpose.

Berulle did much to restore the spirit of religion that leads to the worship of God with due reverence and adoration, and his writings had a profound influence on John's spirituality, and the manner and purpose of his preaching. Berulle taught that through his Baptism the Christian commits himself to adore the divine perfections, the will and judgement of God, and the mysteries of His Son. "This is what we must do all our life because it is the first thing that God commands us and, as Our Lord says, it contains all the law. Our love for God should be so great that we should love nothing but Him and for Him… Christians unite this relationship with God to the mysteries of Jesus that are ever present in their effect and will never pass away." One is reminded that the Church concludes her Eucharist Prayer, "Through Him, with Him, in Him, in the unity of the Holy Spirit, all honour and glory is yours, almighty Father, for ever and ever."

This theme was later developed by Saint John Eudes, 1601-1680, who wrote, "We must use our days and years in cooperating with Jesus in the divine task of completing His mysteries in us." Saint John Baptist de La Salle likewise recommended to his followers the practice of uniting themselves, their prayers, work, even their relaxation, and their assistance at Holy Mass to "the merits and dispositions of Jesus Christ, the Victim immolated for the glory of the Father." Berulle was, incidentally, friend and confessor to Queen Henrietta, wife of the hapless King Charles I of England, and he opened an early Oratory in London, but this did not long survive his return to France. The process for his beatification was interrupted by the Jansenist controversy and never resumed, but his benign influence lived on.

Knowledge of scripture

John depended on other writings but he was no mere copyist and, whatever he may have lacked in conventional scholarship, he made material his own with his personal, unpretentious style. In addition to the writings of Berulle, he had an extensive knowledge of Holy Scripture, especially the Gospels and Epistles where one of his favourite passages was Hebrews 12:22-24:"What you have come to is Mount Zion and the city of the loving God, the heavenly Jerusalem where the millions of angels have gathered for the festival, with the whole Church in which everyone is a first-born son and a citizen of heaven. You have come to God Himself, the supreme Judge, and been placed with spirits of the saints who have been made perfect; and to Jesus, the Mediator who brings a new covenant."

He found great support in his prized collection of *Sermons* by Father Jean Le Jeune who had been one of Berulle's disciples at the Oratory, and greatly admired by Saint Benedict Joseph Labre mentioned earlier as a receiver of Vianney hospitality. The Fathers of the Church, especially Saints Jerome and Augustine, gave guidance as did *The Holy Ladder* by Saint John Climacus, Saint John Cassian's *Conference of the Fathers in the Desert*, Fleury's *Ecclesiastic History*, and Rodriguez' *The Practice of Christian Perfection*. John also knew the lives of the saints almost by heart, and every evening he refreshed his memory by reading about the Saint whose feast it was next day and would be the subject of his homily at Mass.

Preparing his sermons

He spent long hours in the cold sacristy preparing his sermons with meticulous care, pausing only to go and pray before the Blessed Sacrament. Composition did not come easily to him and required an enormous effort. What he wrote he learned by heart and, late on Saturday nights he rehearsed his delivery aloud in the graveyard, sometimes to the alarm of passers-by. It is not surprising that the memory failed occasionally, since he had been up half the might learning a script, worn out by the effort, undernourished, and still fasting at eleven o'clock on Sunday morning. As he became more experienced, he found it was not necessary to write every word of his sermons, but he never stopped preparing them with the utmost care. With confidence came the skill to adjust and improvise, and it was then that he discovered himself as a preacher. As the years passed, the severity of tone moved to a gentler reminder of the dogma of Divine Mercy, so that all should be aware of the personal and unconditional love that God has for them.

Call to conversion

He knew precisely what he was doing when he established priorities and, through his sermons and the example of his life, he transformed what had been the least regarded parish in the diocese into a model that attracted pilgrims from all over the world. He spoke so spontaneously from a heart full of love for God and neighbour that many listeners were moved to tears. "My children", he used to say, "as soon as one sees a small stain on one's soul, one must act like a person who takes care of a crystal globe. If he sees it has become dirty, he sponges it to make it clean and shining. My children, it is like a person with a slight illness. He does not need a doctor because he can get well on his own. If he has a headache, he can go to bed. But if it is a serious illness, he needs the doctor and then medicine. When one falls into grave sin, one needs the doctor who is the priest, and the medicine which is confession." In 1845, the distinguished Dominican, Henri Lacordaire, 1802-1861, who played a significant role in the revival of Catholicism in France after the Revolution, responded to John's invitation to visit Ars and he preached at Vespers. The following day John, now fifty-nine, who was preaching at High Mass, joked with his congregation, "You know the saying about when extremes meet. Well, that's what happened yesterday in the pulpit in Ars, when you saw extreme knowledge and extreme ignorance!"

New school: *La Providence*

The elementary school in Ars was open only three months of the year in winter and never in summer because the children's help was needed in the fields and the teacher himself was a farm labourer. John did everything to make sure that their religious instruction was not neglected by using the text of the Catechism when he taught them to read. He substantiated these lessons by holding catechism classes at dawn before work began, and he encouraged punctual attendance by rewarding the first arrival with a holy picture. His preference for single sex education led to his decision to open a school for girls and, in 1823, he selected two parishioners, Catherine Lassagne and Benedicta Lardet, to attend a teacher-training course conducted by the Sisters of Saint Joseph at Fareins. With a little money left to him by his father, and with the help of miraculously fortuitous donations, he purchased a house not far from the church and set up the premises for the school that later would become appropriately known as *La Providence*.

John did not charge any fees so there was no shortage of pupils from Ars and the neighbouring villages when the school opened. The enterprise was blessed with such success that he extended the premises to accommodate a residential orphanage, in which endeavour he acted as architect, mason and carpenter with a happy knack of harnessing enthusiastic help from the villagers. Resources were stretched but food miraculously arrived in answer to his prayers, and money came in from unexpected quarters at moments of greatest need. When there was a particularly poor harvest in 1829, the wheat for sustaining *La Providence* that was stored in the presbytery attic was almost exhausted and the villagers facing a similar predicament were unable to help. John placed the few remaining grains on a relic of Saint John Francis Regis, prayed to him, and then asked the school cook to "Go and tidy up the remainder of the wheat in the attic." She found it full of wheat piled high in the shape of a cone. On another occasion, when there was so little flour left that only three loaves could be baked, he told her to put it into the mixing bowl and add the water. The resultant dough produced ten twenty-pound loaves.

It became John's practice to call into the school every day at eleven o'clock to conduct the children's religious education curriculum and later, when the pilgrimages to Ars became popular, adults joined his classes. The streets outside became so crowded that he had to transfer his lessons to the church where he invariably concluded with a short homily. In 1847, the Sisters of Saint Joseph accepted responsibility for the administration of *La Providence*.

John's devotion to Saint Philomena

From his arrival in Ars, it was obvious that John had a great devotion to Saint Philomena (Gk. 'greatly beloved'), a young girl who had been martyred in the early days when Christians were persecuted in Rome. He built a shrine in her honour, praised his "dear little Saint Philomena" frequently in public, and attributed the extraordinary progress of his mission and the cures he achieved to her intercession. One example is the case of a woman who had to write on a slate to communicate because she suffered from tubercular laryngitis. She was cured when John told her to put the slate on the little altar in Saint Philomena's shrine. On another occasion, when a mother carried her eight year old paralysed son into the sacristy he said, "The boy is too heavy for you. Put him down and go and pray to Saint Philomena". Within the hour the little boy was cured. There were so many similar instances that when people came to Ars asking for his help, he asked Saint Philomena to cure them in their own parishes because he did not want the personal publicity! When he himself contracted double pneumonia in 1843 he attributed his recovery to her intercession.

John was instrumental in the popularity of the cult of Saint Philomena that Pope Gregory XVI authorised in several Italian dioceses in 1835. It was a great joy for him when Pope Pius IX approved a Mass and Office for her feast to be celebrated on 10th August. The Archsodality of the Work of Saint Philomena was founded in 1885, and the members pray for the return of those who may have wandered from the Christian faith, for more vocations to the priesthood, and for the spiritual development of the clergy. They offer their prayers through the intercession of Saint Philomena and Saint John Vianney who was her devoted champion.

Pilgrims come to Ars

In 1823, when John had been in Ars five years, Pope Leo XII succeeded Pius VII. He reinforced the *Index of Forbidden Books* and the Holy Office, and condemned indifference or hostility towards Christianity, Freemasonry, and misplaced tolerance of error and unbelief. He was succeeded in 1829 by Pope Pius VIII whose pontificate lasted only a year. This was long enough, however, for him to further the spirit and policies of Pius VII, and advise against liberal movements in Poland and Ireland that he considered counter-productive. Bartolomeo Cappellari, a monk of the Camaldolese branch of the Benedictines founded by Saint Romuald, who had written a defence of papal sovereignty *The Triumph of the Holy See* in 1799, was elevated to Cardinal in 1826, appointed Prefect of the Propagation of the Faith in 1826, elected pope in 1831 and took the name Gregory XVI. He opposed liberal tendencies in politics and theology, directed the life and work of the Church from Rome, and resisted moves to reform papal government. He was convinced that the independence of the Church necessitated the retention of the Papal States, and on two occasions enlisted the help of troops from Austria to quell uprisings in Romagna. He was not an enthusiast for change, considered the railway a dangerous modern invention, and would not allow its introduction in the Papal States.

Growing reputation for holiness

By 1827, just nine years after his arrival in Ars, reports of John's holiness had spread far and wide, people began to travel from a distance to hear and consult him, he was asked to preach in the churches of neighbouring villages, and invited to conduct missions throughout the diocese. Many remarked on what seemed like an ethereal glow in his eyes when he spoke about the love that God has for each one of us. When he presided at the Forty Hours adoration at Limas, he was embarrassed to discover that bishops and other high-ranking clergy had come to have the benefit of his leadership. He was as mystified by the reasons for his reputation as some of his colleagues who raised questions about his education and qualifications, but he had the unwavering support of his Bishop Devie who told doubters, "I don't know whether he is educated or not, but what I do know is that the Holy Ghost makes a point of enlightening him."

It was not long before pilgrimages began in earnest, with increasing numbers of people coming to have John hear their confessions in the Sacrament of Penance and receive Holy Communion from his hands. By 1830, four hundred were arriving every day, and so extraordinary were his gifts as a confessor that a pilgrim might have to wait several days before it was his turn to enter the confessional where he was spending up to eighteen hours a day. Thoughtfully, the Lyons Railway Company issued cheap weekly returns to Ars, and to this facility was eventually added a daily service of two horse-drawn buses, and two more that met the Paris train at Villefranche. Other pilgrims came on foot, in private vehicles, or in boats along the River Saone, and among them was the Bishop of Birmingham, the renowned William Ullathorn OSB, 1806-1889, who left a graphic account of his experience. He asked John to pray for England and the Catholics there who had a great deal to endure on account of their Faith. John listened with eyes half closed, then suddenly opened them wide in a gaze of brilliance and said confidently, "I believe and am sure that the Church in England will return again to its ancient splendour." Other prelates, priests, monks, nuns, intellectuals, the unlearned, representatives of every level of society, all came to consult him, but he continued to describe himself as "the least important priest in the diocese."

Demanding daily schedule

John began to hear confessions about midnight, stopping at six o'clock in the morning to say Mass. As soon as he had completed his thanksgiving, he started again and was there until half past ten when he recited the Hours of Prime, Terce, Sext, and None on his knees before the altar. At eleven o'clock he gave his customary catechism instruction after which he returned to the confessional. It had become his habit at mid-day to have some lunch at 'La Providence', though this consisted only of some soup or milk with some dry bread, and always taken standing up. Then he made his visits to the sick of the parish, other villagers or visitors, returned to the church to recite Vespers and Compline, and heard more confessions until eight in the evening when he led the recitation of the Rosary from the pulpit. Four or five hours later, he began another day, and this was the pattern of his life for more than thirty years. The routine was more of a daily martyrdom for one who was solitary by nature and inclined to the contemplative life of the Cistercians and Carthusians. In fact, he made several attempts to leave Ars to follow such a calling, but always returned either in obedience to his Bishop's request, or because he was thwarted by crowds of parishioners and pilgrims who had guessed his intentions and barred his way.

The church was packed from morning to night. People queued to receive the Sacraments, knelt in the sanctuary, behind the altar, in the side chapels that had been added to the nave, or on the church steps. Penitents paid substitutes to hold their place in the queue for Confession while they went for food or to the washrooms, and even bishops waited their turn like everyone else. Only the sick and disabled had preferential treatment. With an inexplicable awareness of their presence, John used to open the confessional door and call them out of the crowd. Even in normal circumstances, hearing confessions is a demanding responsibility of a priest's vocation, so it is not surprising that John became worn out by the monumental task he had undertaken, though his sunny disposition did not alter. The church was freezing in winter, baking hot in summer, but for all those hours he sat in a confined space listening to the tales of human waywardness and unhappiness, and giving of himself to comfort to his penitents. He admitted that sin brought him to tears, and not only in the confessional, because he saw it as an assault on God's goodness and could not understand how the human beings created out of divine love, could be so ungrateful and unkind.

An insignificant priest like me

John knew quite well that he was the reason why pilgrims were coming to Ars but he was never overtaken by feelings of self-satisfaction, and was so humble that he was unaware of his own humility. He used to say, "It's a terrible thing to appear before God as a parish priest," and was very concerned that none had been canonised. His virtues were as intuitive as his theology, and he felt that if conversions and miracles took place through the agency of a priest as insignificant as himself, then it was so that the power and goodness of God would be the more clearly seen. He must have suspected, however, that people were regarding him as a saint because they took to snipping pieces off his cassock as he made his slow progress through a packed crowd. His breviary went missing, and when he went to the barber he had to collect the shorn locks and burn them in the fireplace lest they be collected as items of pious devotion. When his portrait was made by stealth and copies went on sale in the village, he said to Catherine Lassagne, "It's me all right this time. I look as stupid as a goose." The portrait, incidentally had managed to capture the impish sense of humour that is so often a characteristic of the saints. He said on one occasion, "The Emperor has done many fine things but he should have made doorways wider so that the crinolines can get through." He silenced a forceful lady giving him the benefit of her advice on how to run the parish with, "We are not in England where Queen Victoria gives the orders. Here it is I."

Good and Faithful Servant

His later years

Much to John's dismay and acute embarrassment, earthly honours came his way. In 1852, Bishop Chalandon of Belley made him a canon of the Cathedral, but as soon as his Lordship left, he sold the mozzetta, the distinctive shoulder cape worn by a canon, for fifty francs and gave the money for the relief of the poor. Three years later in 1855, the French government recognised the magnetism of his appeal and his outstanding contribution to the life of the nation by appointing him Knight of the Imperial Order of the Legion of Honour. Characteristically, he refused to attend the investment ceremony or have pinned to his cassock the cross that no one ever saw until it was laid on his coffin and he could not object.

John was sixty when the conclave of 1846 elected the Cardinal Bishop of Imola as Pope Pius IX whose papacy to 1878 is the longest in history so far. He had a realistic attitude towards political and economic developments in European society, but revolution in Italy and her confrontation with Austria made his position difficult. He could hardly take sides in the dispute, and this made him so unpopular that he had to leave Rome in 1848. To complicate matters, it was the view of the Italians that the existence of the Papal States, extending across the country from east to west, was a barrier to the unification of the northern and southern parts of their country. Pius was able to return in 1850, but only with the help of an Austrian army that suppressed revolutionary government in the provinces, and a French expeditionary force that ejected the new republican party of government in Rome itself.

Our Lady

In the meantime, John was joyfully aware of the surging devotion to Our Lady in his own country, elsewhere in Europe, and throughout the world. In 1830, Saint Catherine Laboure, a Sister of Charity, had received visions of Our Lady standing on a globe with rays of light streaming from her hands, surrounded by the words, " O Mary conceived without sin, pray for us who have recourse to thee," the inspiration for the venerated "Miraculous Medal". In 1846, the American bishops had chosen Mary Conceived without Sin to be the patroness of their relatively young country and, on December 8th 1854, Pius declared the Dogma of the Immaculate Conception of the Blessed Virgin Mary to be an Article of Faith. The Papal Constitution *Ineffabilis Deus* ('The Ineffable God'), endorsed the Church's teaching that the Blessed Virgin Mary was "from the first moment of her conception, by the singular grace and privilege of Almighty God and in view of the merits of Jesus Christ the Saviour of the human race, preserved free from all stain of original sin". This certainty of Our Lady's original freedom from sin in her union with God had been celebrated by feasts in the East and West since the seventh century, and now December 8th is now the date when the universal Church observes the Solemnity. In 1858, four years after the definition of the dogma, Bernardette Soubirous in Lourdes saw a vision of Our Lady who named herself "I am the Immaculate Conception". The doctrine developed in liturgy, art, and piety, and in France the Confraternity of the Immaculate Conception helped lay the foundation for the twentieth century development of devotion to the Most Blessed Virgin Mary, and an appreciation of her role in humanity's salvation.

A good and faithful servant

In 1859, John predicted that death would come to him early in August and, during what were to be the last few months of his life, no fewer than one hundred thousand pilgrims and penitents came to Ars. He had never been other than a parish priest with his pulpit in an unremarkable location, but he told the truth to his parishioners with such simplicity, that people came from all over the world to share in the same benefit. On 28th July he did not feel at all well but at one o'clock in the morning of 29th July got up as usual and went down to the church. During the day the heat became so intense that he fainted several times in the confessional and had to be carried out to get some air. At eleven o'clock he asked if he could have a sip of wine, and when he went into the pulpit to preach, his voice was so weak that he could not be heard, but the congregation guessed that he was speaking of Holy Communion in the Blessed Sacrament because his eyes never left the Tabernacle.

Holy death

Just after midnight, he called Catherine Lassagne and asked her to fetch the Parish Priest of neighbouring Jassans to whom he made his final confession coherently and with humility. He became so weak that those who had come to take care of him slid a proper mattress on top of his unyielding pallet. At three in the afternoon he received the Last Sacraments in the presence of twenty priests who had come to be with him, and he commented to them how sad he was to be receiving Our Lord for the last time. Even in his last hours, people came with Rosaries and medals to be blessed or, with tears, to beg a blessing for themselves, and even though speech was now beyond him, he never failed to make the Sign of the

Cross. At seven o'clock in the evening of 3rd August, his friend Bishop Chalandon arrived, but he could raise only a smile by way of communication. At two o'clock in the morning of 4th August 1859, while outside a storm raged as though Satan was venting frustration at yet another overwhelming defeat, John gently breathed his last. The life of extraordinary self-denial and sacrifice, devotion, prayer, charity, patience, humility and mortification had drawn to a close. He had fought the good fight, finished the course, and was now receiving his crown. Those present say "his venerable face was sweet and calm as if he were having a quiet sleep." At dawn on the day of his funeral, about seven thousand mourners, among them many priests and bishops, gathered in or near the village of Ars for the funeral procession. Before John was carried into his church, Bishop Chalandon gave a salutary reminder of the power of the saints to intercede for us, all the more because they are now in heaven: "The apostolate of the saints does not end with their earthly life."

Changing times

John was spared the temporal upheavals that marked the remaining eighteen years of Pius IX's papacy. The Pope saw his sovereignty over the Papal States, the 'Patrimony of Saint Peter', dwindle as one church province after another chose to join the new Italian nation. Even the city of Rome, now deprived of French protection, became part of the Kingdom of Italy. The 'Roman Question' regarding the sovereignty of papal territory remained unresolved until 1929 when the Vatican was recognised as a separate state. Given the political and economic changes sweeping over Europe, it is not surprising that Pius became cautious and politically conservative, countering modernity and some emerging scientific and religious developments with an emphasis on traditional doctrine. In contrast to the nineteenth century's enthusiasm for shared political power, he centralised the Church and asserted his own authority over that of other bishops. He called the First Vatican Council, 1869-1870, that approved two dogmatic constitutions: *Dei Filius* ('The Son of God') on the relationship of reason to faith, and *Pastor Aeternus* ('The Eternal Shepherd') on the papacy's juridical primacy and the infallibility of its teaching office. Papal infallibility was thus defined: "When the Roman Pontiff speaks *ex cathedra* (from the seat of authority), that is, as pastor and teacher of all Christians in virtue of his highest apostolic authority he defines a doctrine of faith and morals that must be held by the universal Church, he cannot make a mistake because he has the divine assistance that Our Lord promised to Saint Peter and with which he endowed His Church."

The dogma of infallibility elicited some fierce reactions. Austria cancelled its concordat with the Vatican, religious confrontation broke out in Switzerland, and a few called "Old Catholics" severed links with Rome and founded their own church. German Catholics had already been disaffected in 1864 when Pius had published his "Syllabus of Errors that censured freedom of speech, and liberal attitudes and interpretations in religious matters. German liberals joined Bismarck in attacking the Church and the controversy, centred in Prussia that had the largest number of German Catholics, spread to other central European states. Despite his unpopularity in some quarters, Pius IX retained the affection of the great majority of Catholics and others who recognised his sincerity, his selfless pastoral care, and concern for the spiritual life of his flock.

Devotion to Saint John Vianney

It has been mentioned that in 1859, the number of pilgrims had reached one hundred thousand, most of them wanting John to hear their confessions. The late Pope John Paul II was one of the modern-day pilgrims who still flock to this remote village where he made history, and from where he continues to show the way to Heaven in the sermons he has bequeathed. After his death, his shining qualities were more widely recognised and he became a popular object of veneration throughout Europe and farther beyond. Pope Pius XI canonised him in 1925, and four years later, declared him the Patron of Parish Clergy throughout the world. At first, his Feast was celebrated on 9th August but later established for the universal Church on 4th August, the date of his death.

The Church prays

Almighty and merciful God, by your grace Saint John Vianney was remarkable for his zeal as a priest and pastor. Help us by his example and prayers to win our brothers and sisters for Christ by love, and to share with them in eternal glory.

From the Gospel of the Feast in which Our Lord urges His followers to pray for vocations to the priesthood: "Jesus made a tour through all the towns and villages, teaching in their synagogues, proclaiming the Good news of the Kingdom and curing all kinds of diseases and sicknesses. And when he saw the crowds He felt sorry for them because they were harasses and dejected, like sheep without a shepherd. Then He said to His disciples, 'The harvest is rich but the labourers are few, so ask the Lord of the harvest to send labourers to His Harvest.'"

Writings: from his
'Catechism on the Priesthood'

With the power of Christ

"My children, we have come to the Sacrament of Holy Orders, a Sacrament that seems to relate to no one among you, and yet relates to everyone because this Sacrament raises humanity to God. A priest is a man who holds the place of God and is invested with all God's powers. Our Lord says to the priest, 'Just as my Father sent me, so I send you. All power has been given to me in Heaven and on earth. Go then and teach all nations... He who listens to you, listens to me; he who despises you despises me.' When the priest remits sins, he does not say, 'God pardons you'; he says. 'I absolve you.' At the Consecration he does not say, 'This is the Body of Our Lord'; he says, 'This is My Body'."

As mediator

"Saint Bernard tells us that everything comes to us through Mary, (the Mediatrix of all Graces); and it may also be said that grace, happiness and all the heavenly gifts are channelled to us through the priest. Through the Sacrament of Holy Orders he places Our Lord in the tabernacle for us, welcomes our soul on its entry into life in Baptism, gives it strength on its pilgrimage, restores it to peaceful calm when death draws near, and finally prepares it to appear before God washed in the Blood of Jesus Christ."

As steward

"What would be the use of a house full of gold, if there were no one to open the door? The priest has the key to heavenly treasures and, as steward of the good God and the distributor of His wealth, he opens the door for us. He does not give himself absolution or administer the Sacraments to himself. He is not a priest for himself, but for us. When we see a church tower we know that the Body of the Lord is there because a priest has been there and has said Holy Mass. If the parish were left without a priest, we could say, 'What can we do in this church? There is no Mass. Our Lord is no longer here. We might just as well pray at home.' Those who want to destroy religion begin by attacking the priest, because where there is no longer any priest, there is no Sacrifice, and where there is no longer any Sacrifice, there is no religion."

Lover of Jesus

"What joy the Apostles felt after the Resurrection when they saw their beloved Master. The priest feels the same joy when He sees Our Lord whom he holds in his hands. The priesthood is the love of the Heart of Jesus, so when you see the priest, think of Our Lord Jesus Christ."

The Mass

It is a comfort to reflect that what Saint John says is totally in accord with the teaching of the Second Vatican Council more than a century later:

"The Sacrifice of the Mass is central to the Faith and life of the Church and her members... God the Father sent Our Lord Jesus Christ into the world and, through His Apostles, He has given the Bishops who are their successors a share in His sacrifice and mission. In their turn, and in varying degrees, they transmit the office of their ministry to priests, deacons and other bishops to conduct the divinely instituted ministry of the Church... By virtue of his ordination, the priest is consecrated in the likeness of Christ, the high and eternal priest, to preach the Gospel, care for the faithful, and celebrate divine worship. He shares the office of Christ the sole Mediator, and proclaims the divine word to all. His most sacred office lies in the Eucharistic worship where he acts in the person of Christ, proclaims His mystery, and unites the aspirations of the faithful to the Sacrifice of their Head. Until the Lord comes, in the Sacrifice of the Mass, the priest makes present and applies again the one sacrifice of the New Testament, the single offering Christ makes of Himself as a spotless Victim to His Father... He brings reconciliation to the penitent, comfort to the sick, and sanctifies the section of the Lord's flock that the bishop has entrusted to him, making the universal Church visible where he is, and sustaining the Body of Christ. As a father in Christ, he takes care of the faithful through Baptism and by instruction. He leads his flock by example in their community that he serves in such a way that it can be called the Church of God" (cf. Dogmatic Constitution on the Church *Lumen Gentium* 28, 1965.

Writings: from his *Sermons*

The eighty-five extant sermons were written for a parish that had been without a priest for some time and had grown lax. John wanted to shake them from their spiritual lethargy and see the reality of their situation. If his words were sometimes disconcerting, it is because he accepted that facing the truth about oneself is not always pleasant. His words remain relevant to any age when Christian tradition is threatened by secular attitudes.

The gift of every day

"Begin your work with the sign of the Cross. Offer your difficulties to God and renew this offering from time to time so that you will have the joy of Heaven's blessing on yourself and all the many things you have to do. Just think of all the valuable acts of virtue you can perform in this way without changing what you are actually doing. If you carry out your work to please God and obey His Commandment to earn your bread by the sweat of your brow, then it has become an act of obedience to His will. If you want to feel true sorrow for your sins, then you are making an act of penance. If, while you are working, you wish to obtain some particular grace either for yourself or for others, then your work has become an act of hope and an act of charity. Every day, we can grow more worthy of Heaven by carrying out our ordinary duties, and doing them for God and the salvation of our souls."

Serving God

"In the midst of life's problems and sadness, it is only in serving God that we shall find happiness and consolation. To serve God, you do not have to leave belongings, parents, and friends unless of course they are occasions of sin. You do not have to spend the rest of your life in the desert weeping for your sins. The father and mother of a family serve God by living with their children and nurturing them in a Christian way, and a servant does not have a problem in serving both God and his master. Serving God as a way of life does not conflict with our responsibilities; on the contrary, it means that they are much better fulfilled."

Laughter

"It is always springtime in the heart that loves God."

Home and family

"What takes place in the home must be in accord with the teaching of the Church so that the souls of children are protected from all harmful influences. Christian husbands! Imitate Saint Joseph by beginning your day's work with God and ending it for Him. Cherish those who belong to you and be their faithful protector just as the holy Foster-father cherished Jesus and Mary."

Prayer

"How often do we come to church without thinking what we are going to do, or say, or ask for, yet when we go and call on someone we have a plan, and have no difficulty remembering why we came. Sometimes it seems as if we say to God, 'I am just going to say a few words so that I can get away quickly!' When we come to adore Our Lord we shall receive everything we need if we ask Him with a lively faith and a pure heart. With a prayer well said, we can command Heaven and earth, and all will obey us."

God's holy name

"God's name is so holy, so great and so adorable that Saint John tells us that the angels and saints in Heaven say without ceasing, 'Holy, holy, holy is the great God of hosts; may His holy name be blessed for ever. When the Blessed Virgin Mary visited her cousin Elizabeth, the saintly woman said to her, 'How happy you are to have been chosen to be the mother of God.' Mary's reply was, 'He that is mighty has done great things to me, and holy is His name.' We must have great respect for the names of

God and never pronounce them in vain but with tremendous respect."

Holy Communion

"Let us try hard to destroy anything that could, in the smallest way, be displeasing to Jesus Christ, and we shall see how our Communions will help us to make greater strides towards Heaven. The more we do this, the more we shall feel ourselves becoming detached from sin and inclining towards God."

Purity

"The pure soul is a beautiful rose, and the three Divine Persons descend from Heaven to inhale its fragrance."

Temptation

"Not to be tempted is the greatest of all evils because then there is reason to believe that the Devil is already regarding us as his property. He concentrates on tempting those souls who are in a state of grace, and those who wish to abandon sin. The rest already belong to him and he has no need to tempt them."

Beware of alcohol

"Take a look at the poor person who is drunk, full of wine and his purse empty. He throws himself down on a bench or table and wakes up in the morning amazed to find that he is still in the tavern when he thought he was at home. Since he has run out of money, he has to leave his hat and coat as a pledge for the wine he has drunk. When he arrives home, his poor wife and children whom he has left without bread, take flight from him unless they want to be ill treated by him as if they were the cause of his problems."

Heaven

"My dear parishioners, we must all do our very best to get to Heaven. There we shall all see God and how happy we shall be. We ought to go there all in procession with the parish priest in front. We must all of us get to Heaven. If some of you get lost on the way, it will spoil everything."

Treasure in heaven

"A Christian's treasure is not on earth but in Heaven, and our thoughts should turn to where our treasure is. We have the noble tasks of prayer and love, and these are our happiness on earth. Prayer is nothing else than union with God, and when the heart is pure and united with Him, it is consoled, filled with sweetness, and dazzled by a marvellous light. In this intimate union, God and the soul are like two pieces of wax moulded into one; they cannot be separated any more. It is a wonderful thing, this union of God with his insignificant creature; it is a happiness beyond all understanding. We had deserved to be left incapable of praying, but God in His goodness has permitted us to speak to Him, and our prayer is incense that delights Him. My children, your hearts may be small but prayer changes them and makes them able to love God."

God's grace

"Just as the earth can produce nothing unless it is fertilised, so we can do nothing without the grace of God."

Christmas Day

"Indeed, we truly believe that Jesus Christ came upon earth, and that He provided the most convincing proofs of His divinity. This is the reason for our hope. We rejoice, and we have good reason to recognise Jesus Christ as our God our Saviour and our Model. In Him is the foundation of our Faith, but what homage do we really pay Him? Does our conduct correspond to all our beliefs?"

Devotion to Holy Mass

"Why is it that having assisted at so many Masses we still remain the same? Perhaps it is because we are there in body but not in spirit... We need never fear that coming to Mass will get in the way of the temporal affairs that await attention. It is really the other way round. Things will go better for us, and we will have more success than if we are unfortunate enough not to assist at Mass... What wonderful happiness it is to have the help of the saints at these moments when we are at Mass."

Devotion to our Blessed Lady

"Let us imitate all the great saints who obtained so many graces through Mary to preserve them from sin. Is it not the case that we have the same enemies to fight and the same Heaven to hope for? Yes, Mary always has her eyes upon us. Do we suffer from temptation? Let us turn our hearts towards Mary and we shall be delivered."

The horror of sin

"Say to God, 'O my God, please give us the grace to detest sin because it is your enemy, the cause of your suffering and death that robs us of your friendship, and separates us from you. O Divine Saviour grant that whenever we come to pray we shall do so with hearts detached from sin, hearts that love you, and hearts that in speaking to you, speak only the truth. I ask for the grace to love you. Give me all the sorrow I should have for my sins; give me the horror I should feel for them so that I may detest and confess them, and never return to them.' My dear brethren, this is the grace that I desire for you."

Charity

"There is no virtue that can provide better evidence that we are the children of God than Charity. The duty to love our neighbour is so important that Jesus put it into the Commandment immediately after that in which He tells us to love God with all our hearts, and stresses that this embraces the whole Law and everything the Prophets have taught. We must regard this obligation as the most universal, the most necessary, and the most essential to religion and our salvation. In fulfilling this obligation, we are obeying all other Commandments. Saint Paul points out that they forbid us to commit adultery, robbery, inflict injury, a bear false witness so, if we love our neighbour, we shall not do any of these because the love we have for him would not allow us to do him any harm.

You might say you cannot endure the faults of your neighbour because he is tiresome. You do not enjoy his company. You love only those who agree with you and share your interests, who never go against you in anything, you make flattering comments about all your good works, and who give you plenty of attention and recognition. You will do everything for such as these and do not mind even depriving yourself to help them. However, if they treated you with contempt or returned your kindness with ingratitude, you would no longer love them. You would avoid their company and be happy to end any dealings you may have had with them. Listen to Saint Paul who will not mislead you. He says, 'If I should give my wealth to the poor, if I should work miracles by raising the dead to life and have not charity, then I am nothing more than a hypocrite.'"

Mischievous gossip

"Many people slander others because of pride. They think that by denigrating others they will somehow increase their own standing. They want to make the most of their supposed good qualities so that everything they say and do will be good, and what others say and do will be worthless. Many irresponsible people cause harm by making comments without bothering to distinguish between the true and the false. Whatever the motive, the reputation of one's neighbour should never be tarnished."

Pride

"Because of pride, we tend to be always satisfied with ourselves but quickly ready to criticise others. There are very few people who do not have a high opinion of themselves, or believe that their own worth excels that of others. If only we felt the need to pray with Saint Augustine, 'My God. Teach me to know myself for what I am and I shall not need anything else to cover me with confusion and scorn for myself'".

Patience

"Another bad habit is impatience, grumbling and swearing. What is the point? Do your activities improve? Do they cause you any less trouble? Is it not rather the other way round? In fact, they cause you a lot more bother and, what is even worse, you lose all the merit you might have gained for Heaven. All the saints have had something to suffer and most of them far worse than we encounter, but they suffered patiently, always subject to the will of God, and soon their troubles were over, and their happiness now will never end. Let us think about this beautiful Heaven and about the happiness God has prepared for us there. If we do so, we shall endure all life's evils in a spirit of penitence and with hope of reward."

Death

"One of the great truths repeated by Holy Scripture and the Fathers of the Church is that one dies in the way one has lived. If you live as good Christians, you will die as good Christians… Occasionally, one may begin badly and end well but this happens so rarely that, according to Saint James, 'death is generally the echo of life'… When all is said and done, no one can say with confidence that he is prepared to appear before Jesus Christ. Yet, in spite of our awareness of this, there are few willing to take a single step nearer to God. My dear children, let us not live like fools any longer because at the moment when we least expect Him, Jesus Christ will knock at our door. How happy will be the one who has not been waiting until that very moment to prepare himself for His arrival."

Our loving Father

"We learn from the lives of the saints that they watched and prayed, but we poor sinners are quite blind in the midst of so many dangers that imperil our souls. Some of us do not even know what it is to be tempted because we hardly ever resist. Who can expect to escape from all these dangers? What consoles and reassures us is that we have a loving Father who never allows our struggles to be greater than our strength, and every time we have recourse to Him, He will help us to fight and to conquer."

Acknowledgements

The CTS gratefully acknowledges recourse to the following sources:

The Documents of Vatican II, Geoffrey Chapman, London, 1966.

The Book of Christian Quotations, T. Castle, Hodder & Stoughton, London 1982.

Christian Quotation Collection, H. Ward and J. Wild, Lion Publishing, Oxford, 1997.

The Divine Office, Collins, London, 1973.

The Sermons of the Curé d'Ars, Henry Regnery Company, Chicago, 1960.

The Sermons of the Curé d'Ars, Tam Books Incorporated, Illinois, 1995.

Dictionary of Saints, D. Farmer, OUP, 1978.

De La Salle, Saint and Spiritual Writer, W. J. Battersby, Longmans, London, 1950.

Butler's Lives of the Saints, P. Burns, Burns and Oates, London, 2003.

The Papacy, P. Johnson, Wedenfeld & Nicholson, London, 1997.

The Popes and European Revolution, O. Chadwick, Oxford, 1981.

Butler's Lives of the Saints, Ed. M. Walsh, Burns & Oates, London, 1984.

Catholic Biographies Vol VII, Catholic Publication Society, New York, 1892.

Dictionary of Saints, D. Farmer, Oxford, 1978.

Portrait of a Parish Priest, L. C. Sheppard, Burns & Oates, London, 1958.

Saints for Now, Ed C. Booth Luce, Sheed & Ward, New York, 1952.

KETO BR

HIGH FAT BREAD

CONLINS ABRAHAM

Content of chapters

Keto Bread

Keto bread is bread that contains low carb; it is made for people who want to burn the excess fat in their body. Keto bread is rich in fat and protein. Keto bread is bread made easy for one to give up carbohydrate bread.

Ketogenic diet:

Any diet that is rich in fat and protein and low in carb is known as ketogenic diet. The short form of ketogenic is what we call 'keto'. There are many keto diets and many foods that help you achieve ketosis in your body. When you eat a lot of carb, the body converts it to glucose which in turn produces energy in the body. Too much carb makes you weighty. For this problem to be corrected, you need the keto diet which is low in carb but rich in fat and protein. Keto diet helps the body to extract fat from energy in your body.

What is the purpose of ketogenic diet?

- It makes you lose the excess stubborn weight in your body.
- You will be able to have a better and healthier living. In other words, you will be healthy.

- You will be able to have your mental functioning clarity. Your brain will function very well. It will be in a very good state.
- It will give you your desired energy to carry out your daily routine.
- It will make you less hungry, it gives you strength and reduce the chances of being always hungry.
- It will lower your blood sugar. There will be no much sugar in your blood.

Things you can eat while on keto diet:

- ✓ Sea food.
- ✓ Fish.
- ✓ Eggs
- ✓ Meats.
- ✓ High fat dairy.
- ✓ Cabbage.
- ✓ Sardines.
- ✓ Vegetables.
- ✓ Natural fat.
- ✓ Nuts and seeds.

INGREDIENTS FOR KETO BREAD

- ➢ Almond flour or coconut flour.
- ➢ Baking powder.

- Eggs.
- Butter.
- Coconut oil.
- Salt.
- Xan than gum.
- Spoon or fork for mixing\
- Oven

MEASUREMENTS:

Measurement with almond flour

6 large eggs.

6 table spoon of milk.

6 table spoon of coconut oil.

12 table spoon of almond flour.

3 tea spoon of baking powder.

HOW TO BAKE KETO BREAD

The ingredients and measurements have been listed above to your understanding. Now we are focusing on how to produce our keto bread. I would like to show you the step by step process in producing your bread. Once you have a free access to an oven, the process is simple and easy to follow and make your bread provided you have all the ingredients at your disposal.

Step1 parboil your egg for about 5-6 minutes (this is just to prevent the bread from having fresh egg taste at the end of your production) for those who will like the egg taste in the bread, you might not bother parboiling your egg.

Step 2 remove the egg and break into a bowl then mix. If you want the bread to be smooth, then you can separate the egg white from the yoke. Mix the yoke now later I'll tell you when to add the egg white.

Step 3 butter and coconut oil.

Use a good butter that is grass fed. You should allow the butter to melt with the coconut oil in a frying pan. Allow it to fry a little so that it will not have any taste. Remove it and add the eggs. Make sure to mix them slowly and gently. Allow them to blend together.

Step 4 Add the dry ingredients into it now that is the almond flour, xan tan gum, baking powder, salt and other spices. Put them into a bowl, mix them together.

Mix all the liquid ingredients and dry ingredients together. You can add the egg white together here and mix them properly with a spoon that will allow you stir it easily. At this stage the bread is ready to be put into the oven.

Little tips: Set your oven heat to about 180°C - 200°C. You should wait until it's fully heated. Put the bread into the oven and wait for about 40minutes before checking it. Checking it before time makes the bread lose its bread shape. It may also reduce in size. After 40 minutes, check if the top is brown then you can remove it. If not let it stays a little longer. Even if its brown you need to be sure it's done, to do that, use a stick to Check by putting the stick through the bread if it comes out dry then it's done but if it did not comes out sticky and moist then you have to put it back to the oven and reduce the heat.

Once it's done, remove from the oven and allow cooling, now you can store in a cool place like fridge or freezer for proper preservation for future purpose. The measurement can be reduced if you want a smaller.

KETO BREAD

CONCLUSION:

The keto bread you have just learnt how to bake is a good diet for those who are interested in losing their weight and for those who want to reduce their intake of carb in their body. This is good for your breakfast, you can use it as your fast food when you are hungry and you don't have anything ready to eat. This bread here is low carb bread, it is rich in fat and protein; it is made for you that loves eating bread. You will not miss your usual bread because keto bread will give you rich fat bread. It is good for your consumption, for your friends and family. I usually advice that you make a large quantity that you can reserve for yourself and the family. Try to bake it yourself so you can control your carb intake. The almond flour will give your bread a better taste. You can DOWNLOAD it now or buy and keep it as your guide to baking keto bread.

I want us to learn how to prepare two other keto diets in this book; they are keto buns and keto Oopsie or cloud bread. You are never at a disadvantage taking on ketogenic diet; you can still take anything you choose to eat. I will take you through the step by step process on how to bake them easily. Make sure to use a scale to measure all your ingredients so that you will be able to get the desired result.

HOW TO BAKE KETOGENIC BUNS

Keto buns are low fat buns; they are made with almond flour, eggs, butter and other low carb ingredients (which we will look into later on) for the purpose of increasing fats and protein with low carb. The steps I will be showing you are very easy to follow and to prepare. I will be using these steps in all my books so I want you to follow it and get the best out of it.

INGREDIENTS/MEASUREMENTS

- I teaspoon of salt.
- 8 teaspoons of melted butter.
- Sesame seed (little to be spread on the bread).
- 4 table spoons of baking powder.
- 3 cups of almond flour.
- 6 large eggs.
- 8oz cream cheese.
- 4 cups of shredded mozzarella.

These are the ingredients you should use for your buns preparation. It is very important you weigh them with your kitchen weighing machine so that you can get an accurate measurement.

1. Bring out your baking powder; melt your cream cheese (this could be done in the microwave oven).
2. Add eggs and stir them together, just add the other ingredients like salt, almond flour. Do this on a baking sheet. Add them and mix them up properly.
3. Brush with butter, try and add some sesame seed on top of the buns or any other seed. Though this is optional.

See it below in clearer terms:

METHOD 1

Step 1. Mix all the dry ingredients together, add your eggs and egg white. Your egg should be fresh. You don't have to cook the egg.

Step 2. If you don't want to add the egg white, you can see good soft buns. You can use boiling water to mix the dough together. Add the psyllium husk powder here and mix everything together.

Step 3. Cut now to your baking sheet.

Step 4. Heat your oven to 180^{0c} , place your buns into the oven.

METHOD 2:

Step 1. Bring out your bowl and all your ingredients.

Step 2. Mix all the dry ingredients together.

Step 3. Add the wet ingredients together, the eggs and the water are the wet ingredients.

Step 4. Use a mixer to mix, be sure the mixture remains thick for a buns is known by its thickness, Cut to shape. Make sure to give them space.

Step5. If you want to add any seed on the buns you can add that now on top of the mixed buns. Put the buns in the oven and leave it in the oven for about 40 minutes. Later check the buns to know if it's done.

Step 6. Remove from the oven and allow it to cool down so you can be able to eat it. You can eat it when it's warm.

The direction above can be better with the psyllium husk powder.

I do advice people to bake more buns so that they can preserve it in the fridge or freezer. Keeping it in the freezer preserves it for a longer period than fridge.

OOPSIE (cloud bread)

THE Next diet I want to introduce to you is the cloud bread or oopsie bread, we should list the ingredient before we bake the bread, this is a delicious keto diet, and it can be use as one of your breakfast meal before you go to work. It is rich in fat and protein; always use it as your break fast diet

1 2 table of spoon of baking powder

2 2 table of spoon psyllium husk powder

3 12 eggs

4 2 spinach

5 2 tomatoes

6 18 table of mayonnaise

7 10 02 bacon

8 4 02 lettuce

9 1 table of spoon cream

Use fresh oil on it. It is very good

INSTRUCTION

1. HEAT YOUR OVEN TO 180C

2. BRING OUT YOUR BOWL AND PUT YOUR EGGS INTO THE BOWL, DON'T PLACE THE EGG WHITE and THE yolk together make sure that you separate the egg white and the egg yolk into different bowl. The eggs should be in different bowl.

3. Beat the egg white very well until it is very stiff, it will look strong as you beat it the salt, it is easier with electric hand mixer, the egg white will stiff to the bowl where you are mixing it as you mix it with salt

4. In the other bowl where the egg yolk is, add the cream, the cream cheese and the baking powder together with the egg yolk and mix every together

5. Now we go back to the place where the egg white is, bring the egg white and add it to where the egg yolk is in the bowl and mix everything together.

6. Put the dough in a baking tray, put a baking powder into it or a paper on it before you will put it to the oven, bake it for about 30 minutes, go and check it if it is done, it will be golden red

7. Remove it and allow it to cool down, store the remaining part in the fridge, you can decide to bake   a larger quantity and keep it in a container and keep it in the fridge for 12 days.
8. It is use to eat egg at home ,you can also use it to prepare BLT diet together

EGG, VEGETABLE AND FRIED COCONUT OIL

Another delicious keto meal you can eat is the eggs and vegetable when it is fried it is a very good meal when fried with coconut oil. This meal can be use for your breakfast meal. It is determination to live the ketogenic lives that make you to succeed in it; you will want to know all the diet that you can eat.

INGREDIENT

1 5 EGGS

2 SPICES SALT AND OTHERS

3SPINACH 1 TEASPOON

4 GREEN BEANS

5 CAULIFFOWER

6 4 TABLE OF SPOONS COCONUT OIL

INSTRUCTION

1. Heat up your fire and put your frying pan on the fire and your coconut oil to the frying pan to heat
2. Add your cauliflower and broccoli or any of the both, add the vegetable on the fire inside the

frying pan you are using to cook, allow it to melt
down within a minute with the other ingredient

3. Add the eggs and mix it gradually with your spoon
4. Add your spices,salt,pepper and spinach
5. All the ingredient you want to put has been added,
   use the table spoon to stir together and watch it
   until it is done that you are ready to eat
6. Remove it from the fire and allow it to cool down
   before you should serve yourself and enjoy it.

That is all the direction you need to fry this meal, it
is very easy and simple diet.

BASSED SALT PIZZA, MENTZA

THIS is another keto diet I want to introduce to you, it is also delicious and good for breakfast, and we actually call it keto breakfast meal. This one can be modify that is why we say it is very easy to make, you can add the ingredient that you want add to it like your onion, vegetable, and different types of cheese to make it more delicious.

INGREDIENT

Garlic powder, selsa, baron, beef, spices

INSTRUCTION TO FOLLOW

Cut your bacon, onion, meat into smaller pieces and keep them in separate plate in the kitchen

1. Bring out your bowl
2. Put the cut onions, bacon and meat in the bowl
3. Add the cheese powder into it and mix it together
4. Spread your bacon on top of it in the bowl
5. Heat your oven to 180c
6. Put the ingredient into the oven and leave it for 35 minutes to done

7. Remove it from the oven and allow it to cool before eating it or serving yourself

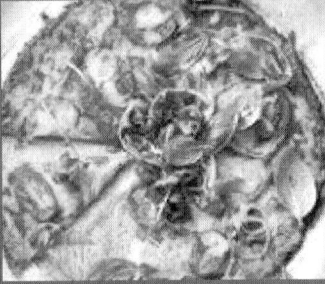

Bassed salt pizza meatza

MUFFINS are snacks that are very delicious that will help you to kill those sugars thirsting desire in you, every one love the keto muffin chocolate because it is very delicious, these muffin are easier to bake than other cookies.

INGREDIENT

$\frac{1}{4}$ cup erytritol (so nourish)

1 cup of almond flour

40g of almond milk (unsweetened)

1table of spoon of baking powder

2eggs

40g of butter

1 teaspoon of vanilla

1 teaspoon of salt

50g of dark chocolate (unsweetened)

DIRECTION

1. heat the oven to 180c
2. mix all your dry ingredient together, the almond flour, baking powder together in a bowl

3. break the eggs into the bowl,mix everything very well until it is well mix and combined together
4. melt the butter and mix it into the almond flour bowl
5. Add the remaining ingredient into it, leave the chocolate apart, don't put it yet and pour it into your button muffin tray.
6. Add the chocolate into it by cutting it into different pieces of small sizes, and place it in the muffin, put 2 to 4 chocolate in one muffin, that means you can make it 2 in one muffin button or 3 or 4 inside it.
7. You can bake it for some minutes,25 minutes
8. Check it and remove it, allow it to cool down before serving it. Enjoy yourself

It is very simple to bake; you can do that by yourself. The recipes is for only 6 muffin

The muffin we just bake is a muffin with chocolate I want us to bake another muffin without chocolate, let's see how it goes.

INGREDIENT

18 o2 cream

8 table spoon of butter

12 eggs

4 scoops

DIRECTIONS

1. Melt your butter on a frying pan, mix it with your cream cheese in a bowl
2. Add the eggs into the bowl
3. Mix it very well, you can use your hand mixer to mix it very well
4. Put the dough into a muffin baking tray
5. Heat up your oven for 180c and place your dough into it and leave it for 25 minutes
6. Check it if it is done and remove from the oven, you can serve yourself when it is cool

Keto muffins with chocolate

Meto muffins

This is keto bagels, it is a low carb diet that you can eat anytime and you can take it any where to eat. It is very easy to bake. Just follow the simple step I will be showing you how to bake this simple diet.

INGREDIENT FOR BAKING BAGELS

Cream cheese

Baking powder

Eggs

Almond flour

Protein powder

Mozzarella cheese

INSTRUCTION

1 large egg

11/4 cup of almond flour

1 table of spoon baking powder

½ cup mozzarella cheese

1 table spoon of fiber

02 Cream cheese

How to bake bagels

1. Melt the cheese on a stove
2. Add the egg and mix it together
3. Add the almond flour and baking powder and combined everything together and let it mix up very well
4. When it is well mix up, it will look sticky in your hand
5. Add oil in your hand while you separate the dough in different portion, roll it like snakes shape in circle by pinching the ends.
6. Heat the oven to 180c and place the dough in a baking tray or parchment cookies sheet
7. Put it in the oven and leave it for about 15 minutes.
8. Check dough if the outside color turn brown, remove it from the oven
9. Allow it to cool down before eating it

Keto bagels

CONCLUSION

The keto bread in this books and other diets are simplified for you to know how to make or bake them without you having any difficulty during the process, it is also for you to have multiple choices of what to eat for your ketogenic diet. You are the determiner of how fast your body gets to ketosis, what you do and what you take in is very important for you to get into ketosis. With your delicious keto bread, buns and other diet, you can replace your carb diet with this ketogenic diet and take them with you to work so that you can enjoy them any time you are hungry. Bake larger quantity of your bread and snacks and store them in the fridge or freezer so that you can make do with them when you are hungry.Ketones are produce when you adapt into ketosis and insulin production will reduce, your body will become a fat burning marching, which will result to loss of weight, freedom from diabetes and you will enjoy other glorious benefit you stand to enjoy in keto diet beyond what was mention in the beginning of this book. Take this book and use it as your pocket manual   at all time.

ABOUT THE AUTHOUR

He is a nutritionist and a writer

,CONLINS ABRAHAM

Printed in Great Britain
by Amazon